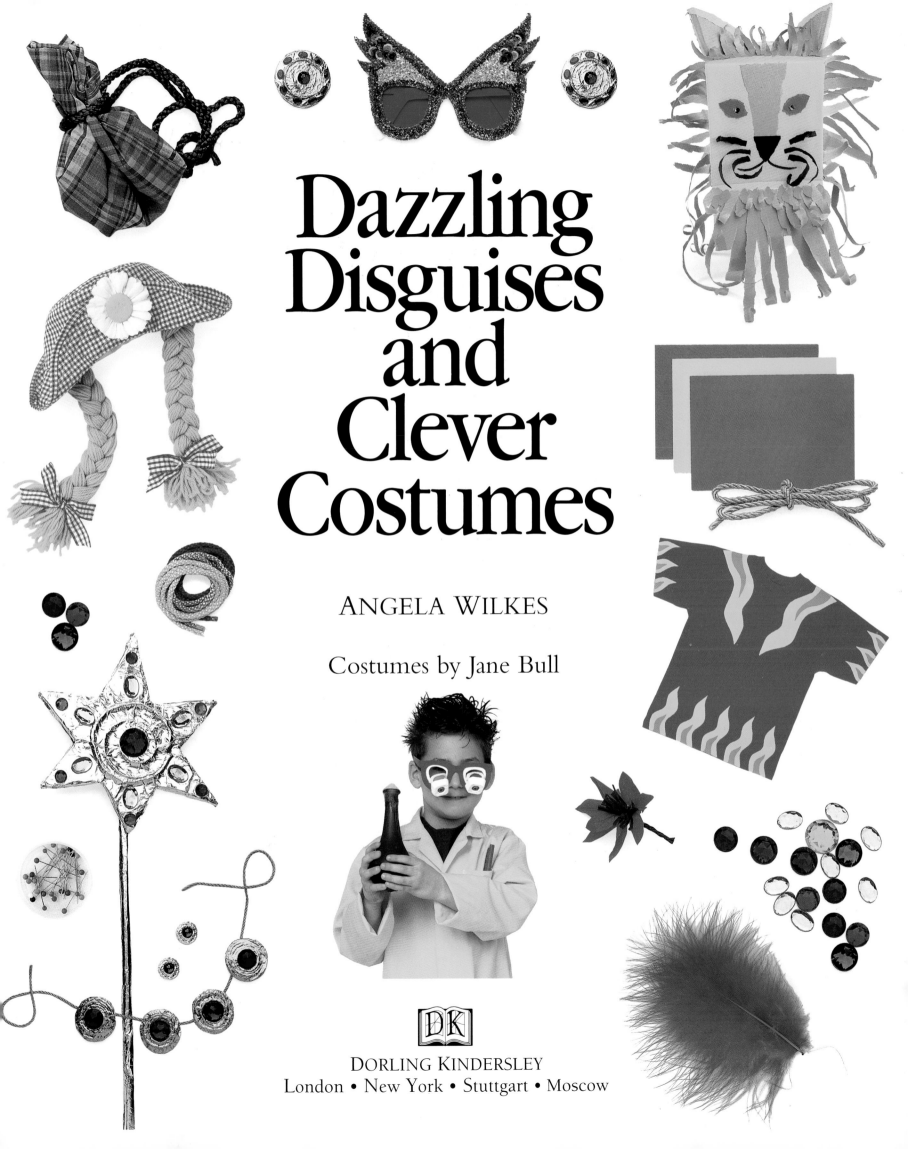

# Dazzling
# Disguises
# and
# Clever
# Costumes

ANGELA WILKES

Costumes by Jane Bull

DK

DORLING KINDERSLEY
London • New York • Stuttgart • Moscow

**DK**

*A Dorling Kindersley Book*

**Designer**   Adrienne Hutchinson
**Assistant Designer**   Joanna Malivoire
**Photographer**   Dave King

**Editor**   Victoria Edgley
**Managing Editor**   Jane Yorke
**Managing Art Editor**   Chris Scollen
**Production**   Katy Holmes

First published in Great Britain in 1996
by Dorling Kindersley Limited
9 Henrietta Street, London WC2E 8PS

A CIP catalogue record for this book
is available from the British Library.

ISBN: 0-7513-5479-1

Colour reproduction by Bright Arts, Hong Kong
Printed and bound in Italy by A. Montadori Editore, Verona

Dorling Kindersley would like to thank Adrienne Hutchinson and
Joanna Malivoire for creating additional costumes, John
Hutchinson for glasses template, Chris Branfield for jacket design,
Andy Crawford for additional photography and Carey Combe,
Anne Marie Ryan, and Dean Price for their help in producing this
book. Dorling Kindersley would also like to thank the following
models for appearing in this book: Ellisha Akhtar, Montana
Burrett-Manning, Micheal Busby, Olivia Busby, Samantha Cobb,
Holly Cowgill, Lawrence King, Sam King, Taskin Kuyucuoglu,
Tolga Kuyucuoglu, Kim Ng, Sam Priddy, Tabedge Ricketts,
Tim Shaw, Darren Singh, and Danielle Smith.

# CONTENTS

## MASKS AND HEADDRESSES

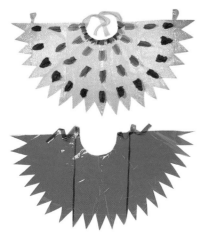

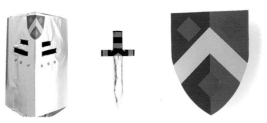

# INTRODUCTION

This book is full of inspiring ideas to help you create a wide range of fantastic costumes and disguises from everyday materials. Below you can see some of the things that will come in useful. Collect as many of them as you can and keep them sorted into boxes, ready for some amazing transformations! Remember, when you finish a project, put all your materials, equipment, and tools away in their boxes, and clean up any mess you have made.

## Things to collect

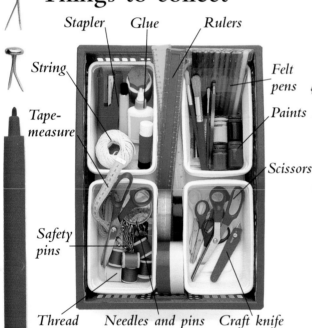

Stapler  Glue  Rulers

String

Tape-measure

Felt pens

Paints

Scissors

Safety pins

Thread  Needles and pins  Craft knife

Long-sleeved shirt  T-shirt

Waistcoat

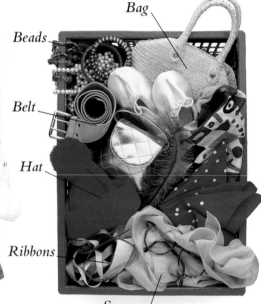

Beads  Bag

Belt

Hat

Ribbons

Scarves

### Basic equipment
Collect as many craft and sewing materials as you can. You will need sharp scissors for cutting out, coloured thread, and different types of glue for card and fabrics.

### Old clothes
Keep old clothes and look for special finds in second-hand shops. If the clothes are too big you can easily cut them down.

### Accessories
You can transform a costume with simple accessories. Collect bags, beads, belts, scarves, shoes, old glasses, and coloured ribbons.

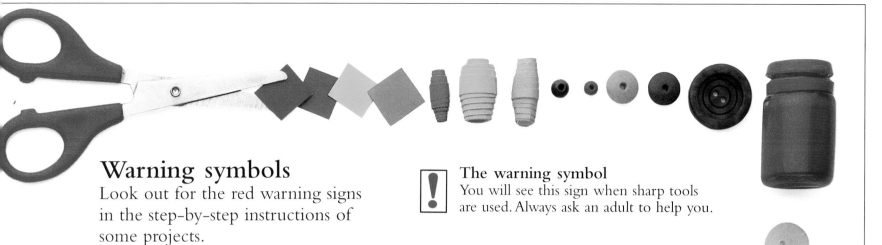

## Warning symbols

Look out for the red warning signs in the step-by-step instructions of some projects.

**The warning symbol**
You will see this sign when sharp tools are used. Always ask an adult to help you.

## Seeing stars

At the top of each page you will find a star symbol that tells you how long the most difficult project on each page takes.

**One star**
☆ Project takes an hour or less to complete.

**Two stars**
☆☆ Project takes an afternoon to complete.

**Three stars**
☆☆☆ Project takes a day or more to complete.

Cardboard tubes   Egg carton

Foil

Plastic bottle

Wire

Bubble-wrap

Plastic packaging   Cardboard boxes

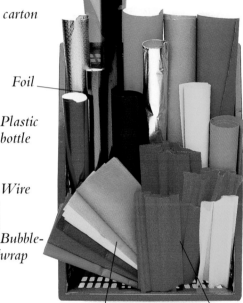

Tissue paper   Crêpe paper

Ball of wool   Lining material

Fur fabric

Old towel

Old curtain

## Scrap box

Save boxes and clean pieces of rubbish for recycling into costumes. Cardboard tubes, egg cartons, old decorations, and plastic lids are all very useful.

## Paper collection

Collect paper and card in different thicknesses and colours. The more you have, the better. Try to include some shiny foil paper and coloured cellophane.

## Fabric box

Save scraps of fabric and leftover balls of wool. Old tablecloths, towels, and sheets are useful, and so are curtains.

# BOX MASKS

Here and overleaf you can find out how to make amazing lion, bird, and insect masks out of cardboard boxes. For each mask you will need a strong, light box that fits over your head as far as your shoulders. Below, you can see how to make it fit properly so it doesn't slip when you wear it. Save interesting pieces of packaging to create features for the masks.

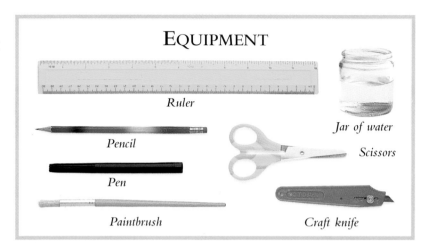

## EQUIPMENT

Ruler

Jar of water

Pencil

Pen

Scissors

Paintbrush

Craft knife

## You will need

Strong glue

Glue stick

Masking tape

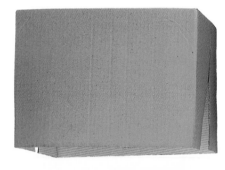

Coloured paper

Pieces of packaging

Cardboard boxes

Sticky tape

Coloured tissue paper

Paint

## The basic box mask

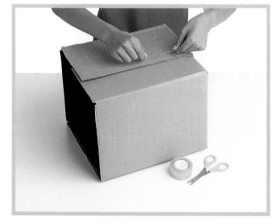

1 Cut the flaps off the box (keep one flap for the lion mask). If the box is too long from front to back, cut it in half, as shown.

2 Slide one half of the box over the other until the box fits your head. Firmly tape the two halves together where they overlap.

3 Try the box on and feel where the eye-holes should be. Take the box off, mark the spots with a pencil and cut out two holes for your eyes.

# Wild lion

1 Leave one flap on the box. Cover the flap and front of the box, half of the top and sides with yellow paper, folding it and gluing it in place.

2 Cut two ears out of cardboard and fold them in half. At the base of the ears bend back tabs and tape them to the top edges of the box.

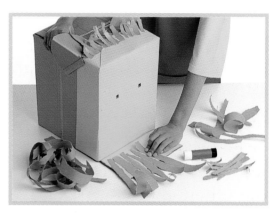

3 Tear up some short and long strips of orange and brown paper. Glue them to the front flap, top, and sides of the box, to make a mane.

# Exotic bird

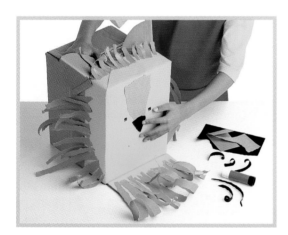

4 Tear out pieces of coloured paper to make a nose strip, nose, eyes, and whiskers. Glue them to the box and then draw on a mouth.

1 Cover the back, top, and sides of a box with blue paper. Draw a bird's crest on thick card, cut it out and cover it with yellow paper.

2 Make short cuts every 3 cm along the bottom of the crest. Fold them back to make tabs and tape them to the top of the box.

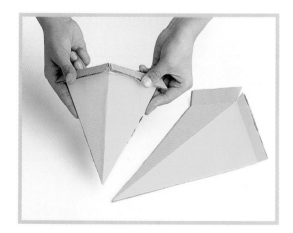

3 For a beak, cut out two triangles of card, one longer than the other. Cover them with yellow paper and fold in half. Bend tabs at the ends.

4 Tape the beak tabs to the box. Gather several pieces of blue and lilac tissue paper, and tear out feather shapes.

5 Glue the paper feathers to the box, working forwards from the blue paper. Glue two circles of pink tissue paper around the eye-holes.

7

# MASQUERADE

## Evil insect

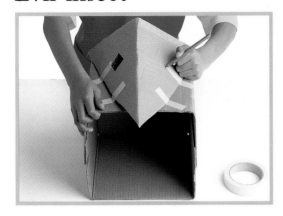

1 Cut three triangular corners of varying sizes off a box. Tape the largest one to the front of the mask. Cut two holes in it over the eye-holes.

2 Tape a corner to the top of the box and the last corner on the back. This corner may need a ball of modelling clay, to act as a weight.

3 Stick pieces of plastic packaging over each eye-hole and cut a hole in them. Paint the whole mask with thick green paint and let it dry.

### Wild lion
The mane for the lion mask is built up by gluing on long strips of paper, then gluing shorter strips just below the face.

### Evil insect
You can vary the insect mask depending on the pieces of packaging you have at home. Anything black or shiny will do. You could even try painting the mask blue or black instead.

*Feelers made from strips of shiny green card with foil cup cases taped to the end*

*Nose strip and other features torn out of coloured paper*

*The mouth is drawn on with a thick black pen.*

*Glue torn strips of black paper around the mouth for whiskers.*

## Birds and beasts

4 Cut out circles of green foil and stick them on to the box. Glue the base of a green plastic bottle to the top of the insect's face.

5 Cut three long strips of shiny card. Slot them through slits in the mask and tape them in place. Decorate the face with foil cup cases.

With a little imagination, each mask can be the basis for a whole costume. Turn to page 44 for some more ideas.

Circle of shiny green foil

Base of a green plastic bottle

### Exotic bird
Choose any colours you like for the bird's feathers. You could make it look like a parrot by using red, blue, and yellow feathers. Or leave out the crest and make white feathers, to create a duck.

Crest made of card covered in yellow paper

Feathers torn out of blue and lilac tissue paper

Eyes made from plastic packaging with foil cup cases stuck on top

Rings of dark pink tissue paper for eyes

Proboscis made from a strip of shiny green card

Blue circles drawn on beak for nose holes

Beak made from card covered in yellow paper

# PANTOMIME HORSE

For a fancy dress party, why not make your own pantomime horse costume that you wear with a friend? The horse is made in two pieces; a box mask for the head, and a fabric body. You can use fur fabric for the body, or perhaps an old blanket or towel.★ Turn the page to find out how to put your costume together and move around in your finished horse.

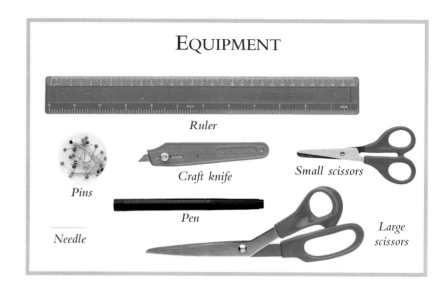

### EQUIPMENT

*Ruler*

*Pins*

*Craft knife*

*Small scissors*

*Pen*

*Needle*

*Large scissors*

## You will need

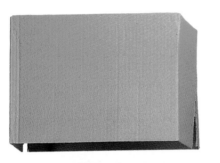

*2 boxes the same size, each big enough to fit over your head*

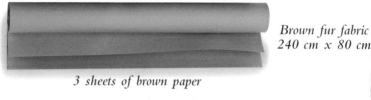

*3 sheets of brown paper*

*Brown fur fabric 240 cm x 80 cm*

*Glue stick*

*Reel of brown thread*

*Sticky tape*

*Black paper*

*2 sheets of black crêpe paper*

*Dark brown, yellow, and white paper*

## Making the head

1 Cut off an end from one of the boxes. Slide the open end of the box inside the other box at right angles. Tape the two boxes together.

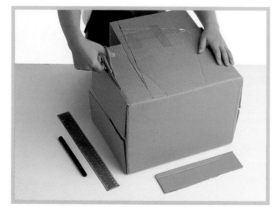

2 To make room for your head, cut a slit on each side of the end of the outside box, leaving a flap at the back. Trim boxes along line shown.

3 Draw and cut out two large ears on the leftover box pieces. Score a line down the middle of each ear with your scissors and fold the ears in half.

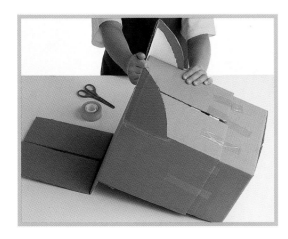

4 Cover the backs of the ears with brown paper and the insides with white and brown paper. Tape the ears to the top back corners of the head.

5 To cover the horse's head, cut out some brown paper to fit the front, top, back, and sides of the box. Glue it in place with the glue stick.

6 Cut two nostril holes at the front of the head to act as eye-holes.★ Glue on pieces of paper for a blaze, eyes, and a strip of yellow as a mouth.

7 To make the mane, fold one sheet of black crêpe paper to a width of 18 cm. Cut narrow strips into the folds, stopping 2 cm from the top.

8 Open out the mane and glue it to the centre back of the head and neck, making sure you leave a piece of mane for the horse's fringe.

9 Fold up the black crêpe paper fringe to fit the space between the horse's ears. Then carefully glue the fringe in place.

## Making the body

1 Fold the fabric in half lengthwise, fur side in, to make a rectangle (120 cm x 80 cm). Place the fold to your right.

2 Cut a curve in the top left hand corner. Start pinning★ the fabric 30 cm from the fold at the top and finish 36 cm from the bottom edge.

3 Sew along the edges you have pinned, leaving a 5 cm hole for the horse's tail marked on the curve. Turn the fabric fur side out.

# HORSING AROUND

## Making the tail

1 Use a folded sheet of black crêpe paper. Cut narrow strips along it, as you did for the mane, stopping 4 cm from the top of the paper.

2 Bunch the tail together and wind sticky tape around the top. Then push it into the hole in the body and secure it in place with tape.

## Making the hooves

Draw and cut four shapes out of thin black card as shown. Bend the hooves until they fit neatly around your feet and fasten the edges with tape.

## Ready to gallop!

It takes a bit of practise for two people to move about in a horse costume. Don't forget that the person at the back can't see where you are going, so walk together slowly before trying to gallop.

### Changing places

The person at the back of the horse can get hot inside the furry body and it's hard work bending down, so do swap places.

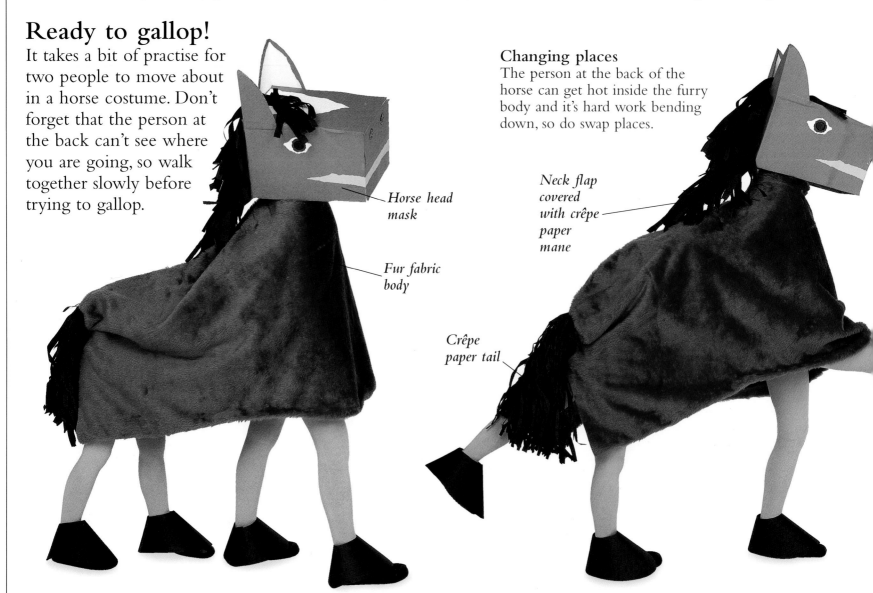

*Horse head mask*

*Fur fabric body*

*Neck flap covered with crêpe paper mane*

*Crêpe paper tail*

# Putting on the costume

**1** Put on your hooves. Your friend puts his or her head through the neck hole. Now help your friend put the mask on.

**2** Pull the body straight and lift it up at the back, ready to put the costume on. Remember to make sure that the tail is untangled.

**3** Bend over and pull the back of the horse costume down over you. Put your arms around your friend's waist and get ready to walk!

**Zippy zebra**
Make the zebra costume in the same way as the pantomime horse. Just use black and white fur fabric for the body and paper for the mask.

*It is a good idea for both people to wear matching leggings or trousers.*

*Bend the card hooves around your feet and fasten the edges together at the back with sticky tape.*

**Pantomime act**
As part of a show, a pantomime horse can really make the audience laugh. Try dancing to music and hopping from one foot to another. End your show by curtseying with both pairs of legs. Try not to fall over!

*White, brown, and black paper eyes*

13

# HATTER'S WORKSHOP

If you want to create a new costume with just one item, make a hat. Tall hats, broad hats, pointed hats, or puffy hats can all be made following the simple methods shown here for cylinder, headband, and cone hats. Turn the page to find out how to decorate the hats and to see the stunning results.

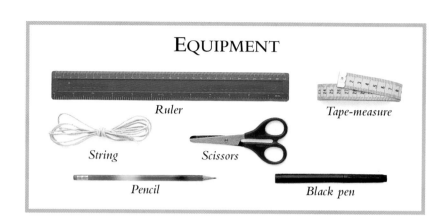

### EQUIPMENT

*Ruler*

*Tape-measure*

*String*

*Scissors*

*Pencil*

*Black pen*

## You will need

*Coloured card*

*Coloured foil*

*Coloured tissue paper*

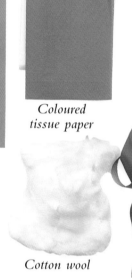

*Coloured foil cup cases*

*Silky scarf*

*Glue stick*

*Cotton wool*

*Coloured ribbons*

*Red tinsel*

*Sticky tape*

*Narrow elastic*

*Strong glue*

## Headband hats

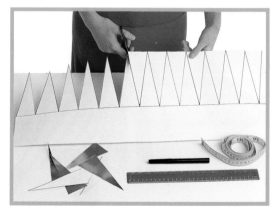

1 Measure around your head. Cut out a strip of card 3 cm longer than the measurement. Tape the two ends together with a 3 cm overlap.

2 To decorate the headband, draw shapes, such as leaves or stars, on the back of the card. Cut them out and glue them to the headband.

3 For a crown, cut a headband 22 cm deep out of gold card. Cut points halfway down the card and tape the two ends together.

# Cylinder hat

1 Measure and cut out a rectangle of card as for a headband, but make it 17 cm tall. Bend the card into a cylinder and tape the edges together.

2 Stand the cylinder hat in the middle of a piece of card and tape it in place. Draw a circle around the bottom of the hat, then untape it.

3 Draw a circle 7 cm outside the first circle and cut it out to make a brim. Cut out a circle 2 cm inside the circle and cut tabs as shown.

4 Fold the tabs up along the line. Place the cylinder over the tabs and tape them in place so that the brim sits straight.

# Chef's hat

1 Cut out a piece of white card like the cylinder hat, then score vertical lines with a pen every 2 cm along the card. Tape it into a cylinder.

2 Cut out a circle of tissue paper larger than the hat and tape pleats around the edge until it fits inside the top of the hat. Then tape it in place.

# Cone hats

1 For tall hats, draw a quarter circle on some card with a pencil tied to an end of a piece of string. Make the string the height you want the hat.

2 Then cut out the hat along the line you have drawn. For shorter hats, like the clown's hat, you will need to draw and cut out a semicircle.

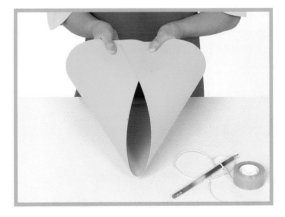

3 Roll the piece of card into a cone, then try it on your head and adjust it until it fits properly. Tape the two straight edges together.

# HATS ON PARADE

## Starry witch

1 To make the notched brim for a witch's hat, cut tabs about 3 cm deep all the way around the bottom of the cone. Fold the tabs up.

2 To finish off the witch's hat, cut out stars and small diamonds from shiny green paper and glue them to the hat and brim.

## Regal crown

Glue foil cup cases around the crown to make jewels. Stick cotton wool on the base of the crown and add tiny pieces of black paper.

## Medieval wimple

1 Cut a hole on each side of a tall cone hat. Thread elastic through the holes. Leave enough to fit under your chin. Secure ends with a knot.

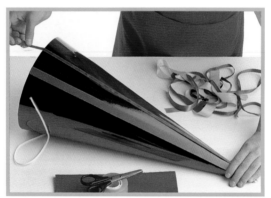

2 Tape coloured ribbons from top to bottom of the cone hat. Then attach a folded piece of tissue paper around the bottom.

## Hat collection

Here you can see the basic headband, cylinder, and cone hat shapes transformed into wimples, wreaths, crowns, and top hats. See how many more hats you can invent, using these basic shapes.

*Silky scarf*

**Clown hat**
This small cone hat is made from yellow card and decorated with red paper spots and tinsel.

**Emperor's wreath**
Based on a Roman emperor's wreath, this headband is decorated with ivy leaves cut out of gold card.

**Witch's hat**
This cone hat has a notched brim and is decorated with foil stars. You could make a wizard's cone hat from dark blue paper and silver stars.

**Magician's top hat**
The magician's hat has a narrow brim and a band of red ribbon around the cylinder. Tuck a toy bunny in the top for an added surprise.

*Tall cylinder*

*Notched brim*

**Chef's hat**
The chef's hat is made from scored white card taped into a cylinder. A puff of white tissue paper is taped to the crown.

**Regal crown**
Decorate a gold crown made from a headband with cotton wool, black pieces of card, and foil cup cases.

*Folded tissue paper taped to the brim*

*Large brim*

*Narrow red ribbon*

**Medieval wimple**
This tall cone hat has stripes made from narrow coloured ribbons and a floaty scarf taped to the top of it.

**Matador's hat**
A short cylinder hat with a very wide brim gives this black paper hat its matador shape.

# SPACE-AGE ROBOT

To create your own robot costume, look for interesting pieces of packaging around your home. The main item is the helmet. You will need a carton big enough to cover most of your head. We used a popcorn carton painted blue, but if you can't find a carton, try a small box instead. Decorate it with bright colours to create a friendly robot, or try using black and silver to create a scary robot.

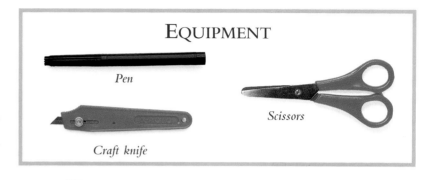

EQUIPMENT

Pen

Scissors

Craft knife

## You will need

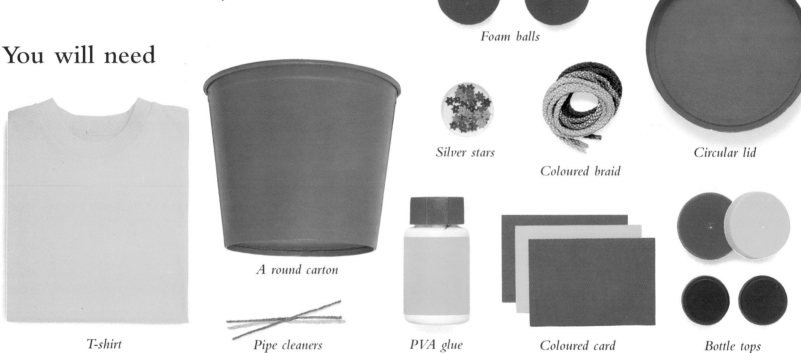

Foam balls

Silver stars

Coloured braid

Circular lid

T-shirt

A round carton

Pipe cleaners

PVA glue

Coloured card

Bottle tops

## Making the helmet

1 Try the carton on your head and mark an eye-hole. Cut a long rectangular slot around the marks so you can see out of the helmet.

2 Stick a foam ball on the end of two pipe cleaners. Make two tiny holes in the sides of the carton and push the pipe cleaners into them.

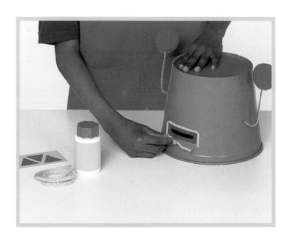

3 Bend the pipe cleaners upwards. Glue card and pipe cleaners around the eye-slot and decorate the carton with shapes of coloured card.

## Decorating the T-shirt

1 Paint the circular lid bright colours and glue a bottle top in the middle of it. Glue short pieces of braid inside the lid, as shown.

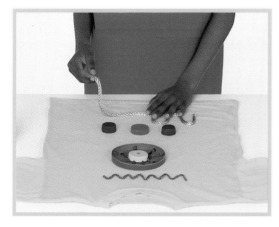

2 Glue the lid in the centre of the T-shirt, to look like a control panel. Stick on bottle tops and wiggly lines of braid to decorate the T-shirt.

## Robot power

The helmet and T-shirt give you the basis for your robot costume. Turn to page 44 for ideas of more things to add to your outfit. Don't forget to move your arms and legs in a stiff, jerky way like a robot!

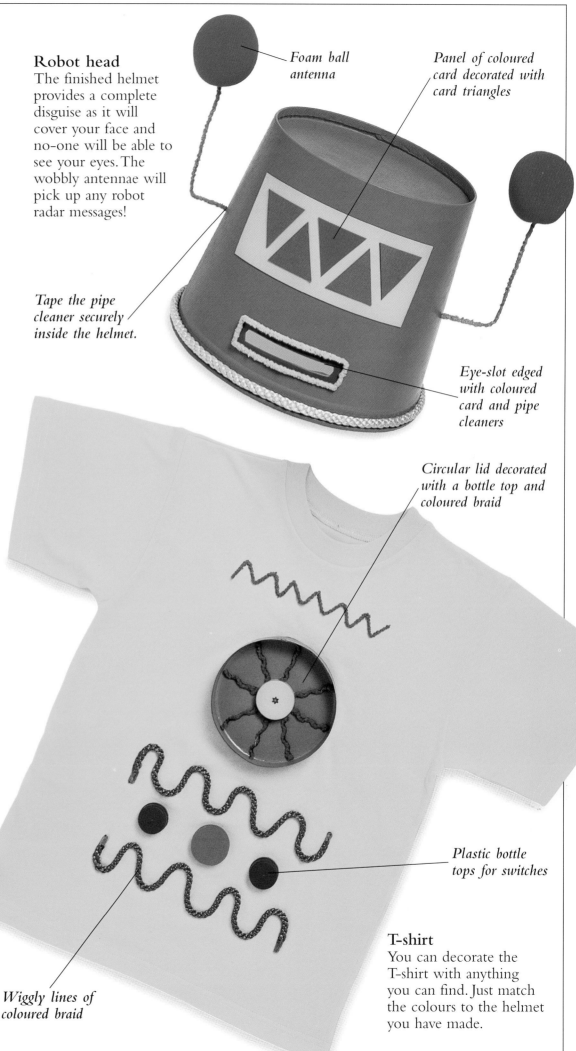

### Robot head
The finished helmet provides a complete disguise as it will cover your face and no-one will be able to see your eyes. The wobbly antennae will pick up any robot radar messages!

*Foam ball antenna*

*Panel of coloured card decorated with card triangles*

*Tape the pipe cleaner securely inside the helmet.*

*Eye-slot edged with coloured card and pipe cleaners*

*Circular lid decorated with a bottle top and coloured braid*

*Plastic bottle tops for switches*

### T-shirt
You can decorate the T-shirt with anything you can find. Just match the colours to the helmet you have made.

*Wiggly lines of coloured braid*

19

# SPOOKS AND HORRORS

Perhaps it's Hallowe'en. It's dark outside, ghouls and spooks are about, and you want to join in the ghostly fun. Or maybe you just want to give your friends a terrifying fright. Here you can find out how to use an old sheet or pillowcase★ to transform yourself into a ghoulish ghost and a grizzly mummy, that look as if they've just stepped out of a horror movie.

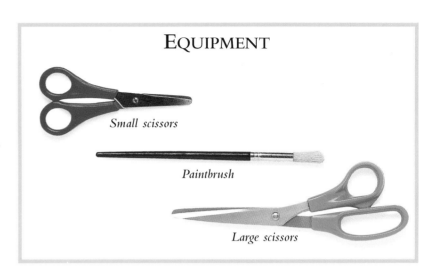

EQUIPMENT

*Small scissors*

*Paintbrush*

*Large scissors*

## You will need

*Large white sheet, tablecloth, or piece of fabric*

*Black felt*

*PVA glue*     *Coloured tape*

## Ghoulish ghost

1 Put the sheet on and mark your eye positions with tape. Take off the sheet and cut out felt eyes and a mouth. Glue these over the tape.

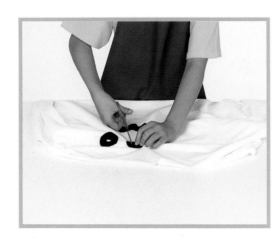

2 Glue the felt mouth below the two eyes. Pinch each felt eye and cut a small hole in the middle of it, through both the felt and sheet.

**Ghoulish ghost**
Practise flitting silently around the house in your ghost costume. Slowly raise your arms and let out a spine-chilling moan.

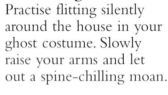

*Black felt eyes*

*Black felt mouth*

*Trim the bottom of the sheet so that it is straight.*

3 Put the sheet on again, with the eye-holes in the right place. Ask an adult to trim around the bottom of the sheet, to make a straight hem.

*★Remember to check with an adult first.*

# Horror mummy

## You will need

*White pillow case*

*Torn strips of a white sheet or cotton fabric*

*Coloured tape*

*Red paint*

1 Put the pillowcase on and mark the position of your face with tape. Take off the pillowcase, cut a face hole and then trim off the bottom.

2 Put the pillowcase back on your head. Ask a friend to loosely wind strips of fabric around your head, to hold the pillowcase in place.

### Finishing touches

Ask your friend to paint a red ear "wound" on the side of your head. Then bend one arm across your stomach so it can be bandaged up. You can also bandage your free arm and hand.

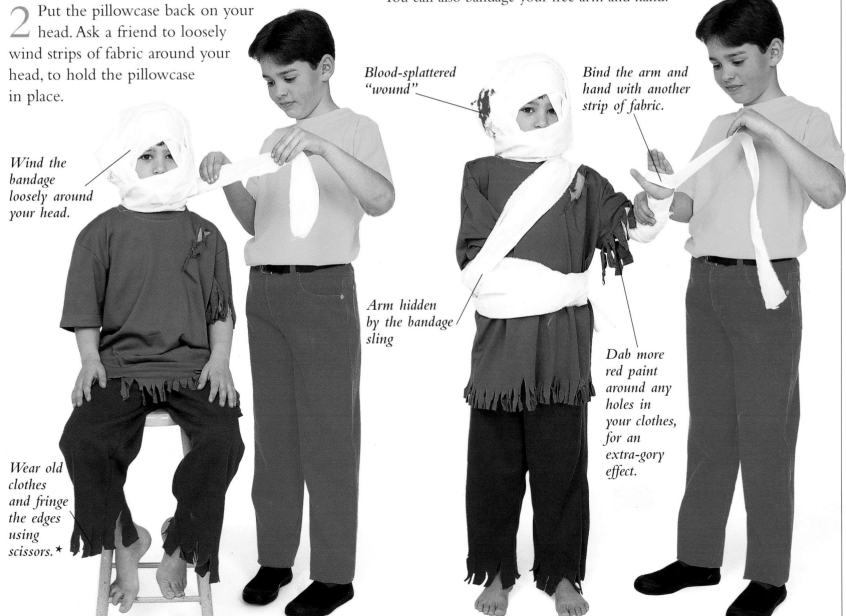

*Wind the bandage loosely around your head.*

*Wear old clothes and fringe the edges using scissors.* ★

*Blood-splattered "wound"*

*Arm hidden by the bandage sling*

*Bind the arm and hand with another strip of fabric.*

*Dab more red paint around any holes in your clothes, for an extra-gory effect.*

# UNDER WRAPS

There are some costumes that are very simple to make and can be invented by playing around with whatever odd bits of fabric you have; old towels, curtains, or tablecloths.★ You wrap, twist, tug, and tie and instantly you are a Roman emperor or a desert island dancer! Big safety pins are handy for these costumes and ribbons, jewellery, and flowers are great accessories.

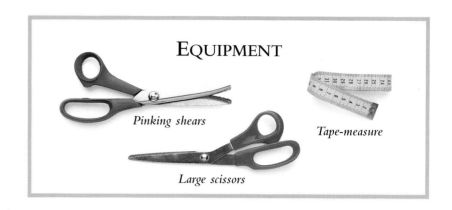

### EQUIPMENT

*Pinking shears*

*Tape-measure*

*Large scissors*

## You will need

### For a sarong

*A piece of flowery fabric about 90 cm x 170 cm*

*Smaller piece of same fabric about 170 cm x 30 cm*

*Crêpe paper flower*

*The skirt needs to be pulled tightly around your waist.*

*Paper flower in hair*

*The material is tied together at the back of the neck.*

*Narrow piece of fabric*

*Tie the fabric in a knot at the side.*

### Sarong

Place the narrow piece of fabric around your back. Then cross the ends of the fabric over your chest and tie them behind your neck. Wrap the large piece of fabric around your waist and tie the ends together at the side.

*Arrange the fabric so that it falls in folds.*

★*Remember to check with an adult first.*

# Start wrapping

Here you can see how to make an exotic sarong, a Roman toga, and a regal turban. All of the costumes are simply made by wrapping pieces of fabric around your body and fastening them in place.

## You will need

For a Roman toga

*Safety pins*

*Brooch and belt (see page 42)*

*Gold ribbon or braid*

*2 large white towels*

*Emperor's wreath (see page 14)*

## Roman toga

Wrap one towel tightly around your waist like a skirt. Tuck in the ends and pin them securely. Drape the second towel over one shoulder and tuck the front into the skirt.

*Gather the towel in with braid and fasten on a brooch*

*Tie a belt, ribbon, or braid around your waist.*

*Towel tucked into belt at the back*

*Towel folds over at the front*

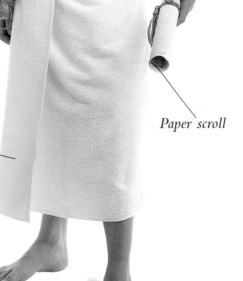

*Paper scroll*

## You will need

For a turban

*A long piece of silky fabric*

*Brooch (see page 42)*

*Twist the ends of the fabric together tightly, as shown.*

## Turban

Wrap the fabric around your head with the ends in front. Twist the ends together, flip them back over the turban, and tuck them in at the back of your head.

*Decorate the front of the turban with a brooch.*

23

# TUNICS

A tunic is a very useful basis for any
costume. Although it is simple to make, it
can be dressed up by adding belts, scarves,
jewellery, or anything else you have
around the house. Here you can see how
to make a royal tunic and a forest archer
tunic without doing any sewing at all. You
can use any type of fabric, and vary your
costume with colours and patterns.

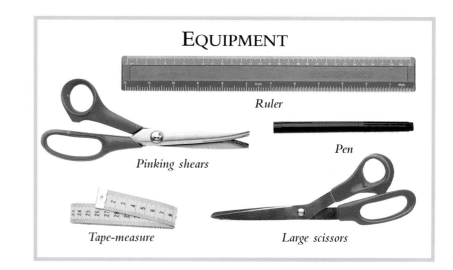
**EQUIPMENT**

*Ruler*

*Pinking shears*

*Pen*

*Tape-measure*

*Large scissors*

## You will need

For the archer tunic

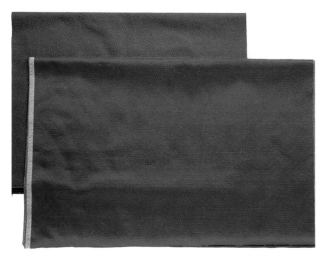

*140 cm x 70 cm fabric for each tunic*

*Pouch made from circle
of fabric tied with braid*

*Narrow scarf or tie belt*

For the royal tunic

*Medallion
(see page 42)*

*Necklace or chain
(see page 42)*

*Wide gold ribbon
or braid*

## Royal tunic

1 Lay the fabric out flat on a table
or the floor, smoothing out any
wrinkles. Measure out a piece 140 cm
long and 70 cm wide and cut it out.

2 Fold the fabric in half lengthwise.
Measure 15 cm in from each edge
on the fold. Cut a slit between the
two marks to make a neck hole.

3 Using the pinking shears, trim
all along the outer edges of the
tunic. This will help to stop
the fabric from fraying.

# Archer tunic

1 Follow steps 1 and 2 for the royal tunic. Then cut a slit 15 cm long in the centre front of the neck to make the collar flaps.

2 Draw deep points along the bottom edges of the tunic, using a ruler and pen. Cut along the lines you have drawn to make a ragged edge.

# Tunic outfits

These two tunics can be worn over T-shirts, or on their own. Tie a scarf, ribbon, or braid belt around your waist or hips and add other decorations to fit the character you are playing. You can vary the basic tunic by making it in different fabrics, or by cutting out a larger piece of material and turning it into a dress.

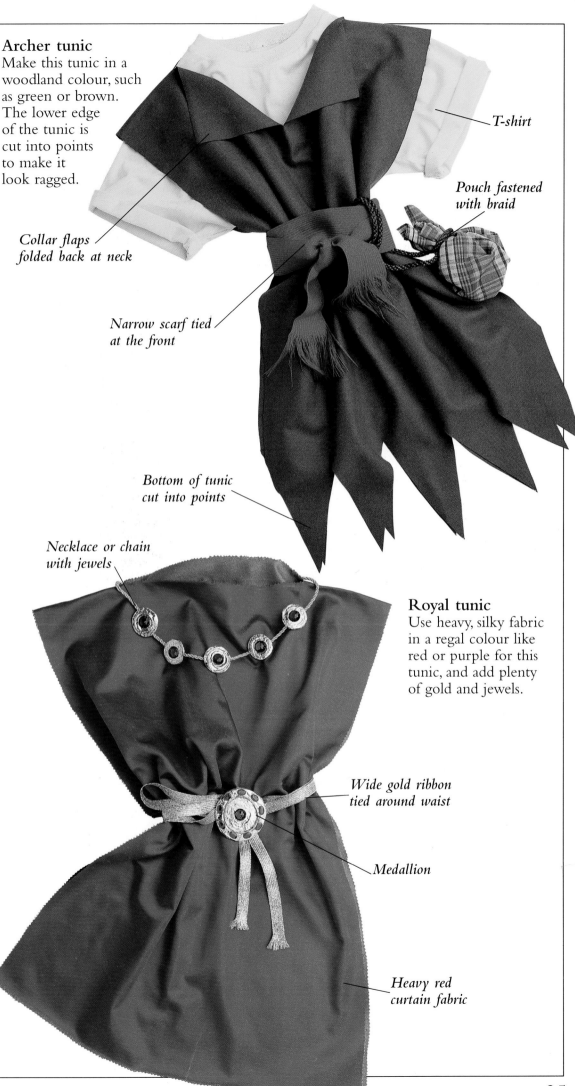

**Archer tunic**
Make this tunic in a woodland colour, such as green or brown. The lower edge of the tunic is cut into points to make it look ragged.

*T-shirt*

*Pouch fastened with braid*

*Collar flaps folded back at neck*

*Narrow scarf tied at the front*

*Bottom of tunic cut into points*

*Necklace or chain with jewels*

**Royal tunic**
Use heavy, silky fabric in a regal colour like red or purple for this tunic, and add plenty of gold and jewels.

*Wide gold ribbon tied around waist*

*Medallion*

*Heavy red curtain fabric*

# TATTERED SKIRTS

You don't need to be a whiz with a needle and thread to make your own costumes. Here you can find out how to make a stunning range of grass skirts using coloured crêpe paper. You can follow the ideas on this page or design your own variations.

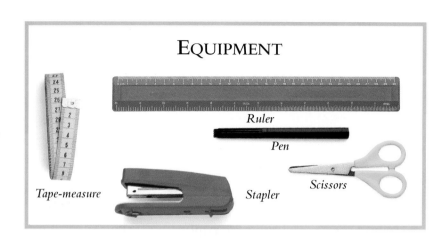

### EQUIPMENT

*Ruler*

*Pen*

*Scissors*

*Tape-measure*

*Stapler*

## You will need

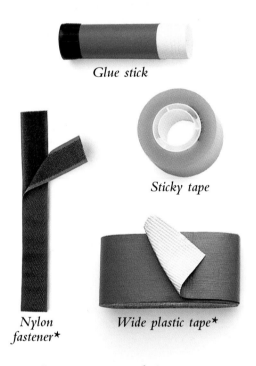

*Glue stick*

*Sticky tape*

*Nylon fastener★*

*Wide plastic tape★*

*Coloured crêpe paper*

## Basic grass skirt

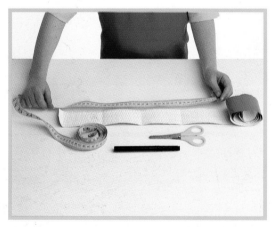

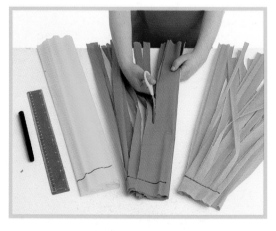

1 Measure around your waist with the tape-measure and add 60 mm to this measurement. Cut some wide plastic tape to the same length.

2 Cut three pieces of crêpe paper the same length as the tape. Fold and cut them, as shown, into thin strips, stopping 25 mm from the top.

3 Stick each piece of paper in layers to the lower half of the tape and fold the top half of the tape back down over them.

## Ra-ra skirt

## Rags and tatters skirt

4 Cover the tape with crêpe paper and decorate it with paper shapes. Staple nylon fastener to each end of the skirt, to fasten it around you.

Make this in the same way as the grass skirt, but shorter. Attach to the tape seven or more layers of crêpe paper cut to different lengths.

Follow the basic grass skirt steps. Use five pieces of different coloured crêpe paper for this skirt, cutting the skirt strips into points.

## Dancing skirts

Choose contrasting colours for your skirt to make a dramatic outfit. Turn to page 44 to see how to use these skirts as part of a costume.

*Waistband decorated with triangles of crêpe paper*

**Ra-ra skirt**
Layered crêpe paper gives this skirt a ruffled appearance.

**Grass skirt**
This skirt is made up of layers of yellow, orange, and green crêpe paper.

**Rags and tatters skirt**
To make this skirt look ragged, cut the crêpe paper into pointed strips.

# CLOAKS AND CAPES

Swirling cloaks and capes are an important addition to many costumes. Kings, queens, witches, wizards, and even birds and insects are enhanced by dramatic cloaks. Here we show you two easy methods for making the cloaks, one for regal robes and the other for a fluttering cape. Turn the page for more ideas.

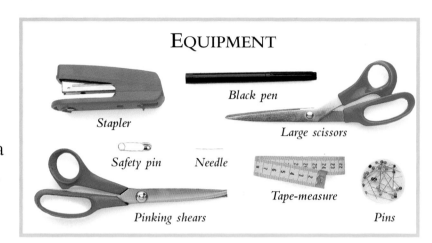

## EQUIPMENT

Stapler

Black pen

Large scissors

Safety pin    Needle

Tape-measure

Pinking shears

Pins

## You will need

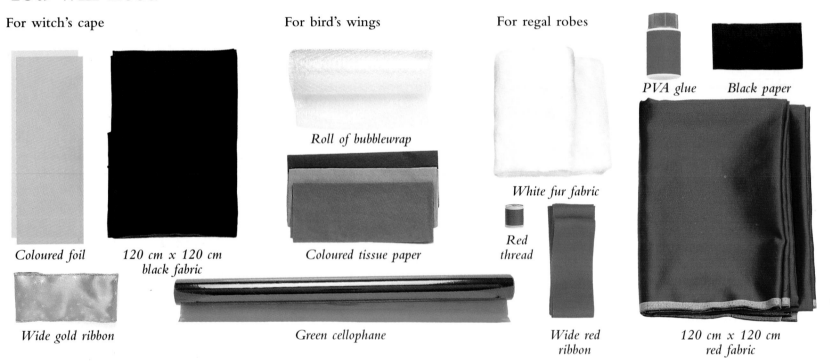

For witch's cape

Coloured foil

120 cm x 120 cm black fabric

Wide gold ribbon

For bird's wings

Roll of bubblewrap

Coloured tissue paper

Green cellophane

For regal robes

White fur fabric

Red thread

Wide red ribbon

PVA glue    Black paper

120 cm x 120 cm red fabric

## Bird wings

1 Tape a sheet of bubblewrap together to make a sheet 160 cm x 80 cm. Fold it into a square. Cut a neck hole and trim the bottom edge.

2 Draw and cut out points along the bottom edge of the cape. Cut two strips of bubblewrap for ties and staple one to each side of the neck.

3 Gather together coloured pieces of tissue paper. Carefully tear out lots of feather shapes. You will need both large and small feathers.

4 Tape the larger feathers on to the cape in rows. Pinch each feather in the middle as you tape it down, to make it stick out a little.

5 Tape over the staples joining the neck ties, to cover any sharp ends. Then decorate the neck edge with the smaller feathers.

6 Cut two long narrow strips of bubblewrap. Bend them into loops and staple to each side of the cape, to make loops for your wrists.

## Regal robe

1 Trim the red fabric. Fold one edge of the fabric, 6 cm wide, over to the back side and pin it in place. This is the casing for the ribbon.

2 Thread a needle with a double thread and knot it at the end. Sew firmly along the bottom edge of the folded fabric, as shown.

3 With pinking shears, cut strips of fur fabric 6 cm wide. Use these pieces of fur fabric to decorate the sides and bottom edges of the robe.

4 Dab glue along the back of each fur strip. Glue the strips of fur on to the front of the robe, down the sides, and along the bottom edges.

5 Cut out lots of small rectangles of black paper. Carefully glue them all over the fur fabric on the robe, as shown.

6 Thread a long ribbon through the folded casing at the top of the robe with a safety pin. Gather the fabric as you pull it through.

# CAPE COLLECTION

You can create your own costume by using different materials and unusual decorations to adapt the cloaks and capes shown here.

*Feathers torn out of different coloured tissue paper*

*Pointed edges cut into the bubblewrap*

*Wrist loop*

**Bird's wings**

Fasten the ties loosely around your neck and slip your hands through the wrist loops. Lift your arms and flap your wings!

*This cape is fastened at the neck with ties.*

**Insect cape**

This cape is made in the same way as the bird's wings, but uses crinkly green cellophane instead.

*Join the sheets of cellophane together with tape.*

*Tie the neck ties in a loose bow.*

## Finishing touches

Here are just a few ways to make your cloaks and capes. To make a wizard's cape, try using blue material and green stars. Why not make the hat on page 14 to wear with the cape, or the king's crown to wear with the cloak? Turn to the Costume Parade on page 44 for even more ideas on what to wear with the wings and robes.

*Broad ribbon gathers the cloak in at the neck.*

*Trim made from white fur fabric and pieces of black paper*

### Regal robe
Choose a dark red or purple fabric for this cloak to give it a truly royal appearance.

*Stars made from coloured foil*

### Witch's cape
To make this cape, follow the pattern for the regal robe but use black material instead. Decorate it with silver and gold stars cut from foil and a gold ribbon.

# MIGHTY WEAPONS

Here and overleaf you can see how to make a suit of shining armour, a sword, and a dagger worthy of the most valiant knight. Everything is made of corrugated card from cardboard boxes and extra-wide aluminium foil. Before you make the breastplate, measure yourself and adapt the armour pattern to fit your body.

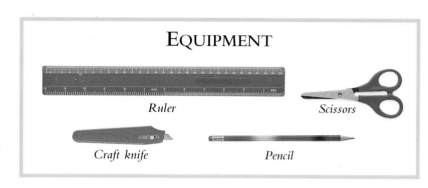

### EQUIPMENT

*Ruler*

*Scissors*

*Craft knife*

*Pencil*

## You will need

*Thick corrugated card*

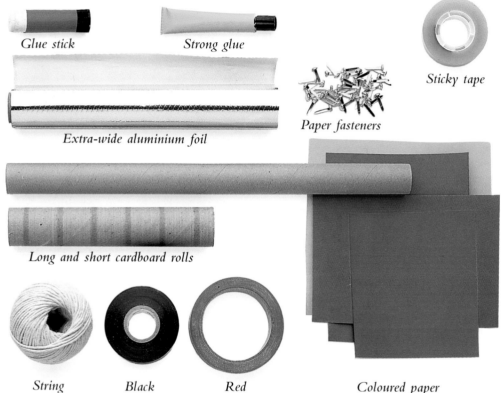

*Glue stick*

*Strong glue*

*Sticky tape*

*Extra-wide aluminium foil*

*Paper fasteners*

*Long and short cardboard rolls*

*String*

*Black coloured tape*

*Red coloured tape*

*Coloured paper*

## Making the breastplate

1 Draw a breastplate pattern on paper, with the neck and arm-holes 20 cm wide. The distance from the neck to the waist should be 37 cm.

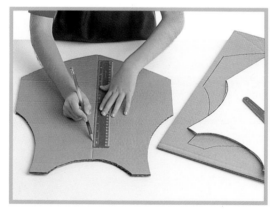

2 Using this pattern, draw and cut two breastplates out of corrugated card. Score a line and make a fold down the middle of each breastplate.

3 Cut out two strips of card 3.5 cm x 40 cm. Cover these straps and the breastplates with foil, taping it in place at the back of each piece.

4 Make two holes at the top of each breastplate. Attach the straps to the breastplates with paper fasteners, adjusting the lengths to fit.

5 Make three holes down the sides of each breastplate. Thread a long piece of string through the holes, as you would thread a shoelace.

6 Decorate the front breastplate with paper fasteners, as shown. Make a paper shield design and glue it to the middle of the breastplate.

## Making the shield

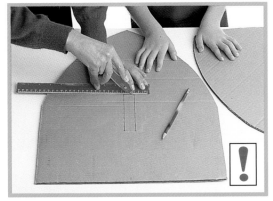

1 Cut two shields out of corrugated card 50 cm x 40 cm, as shown. Cut out a slot 12.5 cm long and 2.5 cm wide in the middle of one shield.

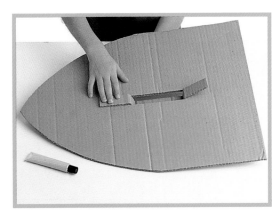

2 Cut out a strip of strong card 2.25 cm wide and 23 cm long. Fold it to make a handle. Push it in the slot and glue the ends in place.

3 Glue the shields together, with the handle at the back. Seal the edges with sticky tape. Decorate the shield with a coloured paper design.

## Making the helmet

1 Cut out a rectangle of card 80 cm x 30 cm. Tape it into a pointed cylinder shape. Make a top for the helmet and tape it in place.

2 Try the helmet on. Then draw and cut out curves along the bottom edge of the helmet so that it sits comfortably on your shoulders.

3 Cut four slits in the front of the helmet, for eye-holes. Cover the helmet with foil and decorate with paper fasteners and a paper shield.

# ON GUARD!

## Weapon blades

Flatten two cardboard tubes, one long and one short. Cut one end of each tube into a point. Tape the ends. Cover the tubes with foil, taping the join.

## Dagger handle

Cut out a rectangle of card 17 cm x 6 cm and make a slit in the centre. Slide the short blade through the slit, fold the card in half, and tape down.

## Sword handle

Cut a piece of card 34 cm x 8 cm with rounded ends. Cover with black tape and cut two slits each end, wide enough to push the sword through.

## Finishing touches

Bend the sword handle as shown. Slide it over the top of the sword. Wrap tape around the blade to keep the handle in place. Decorate with coloured tape.

## Gauntlets

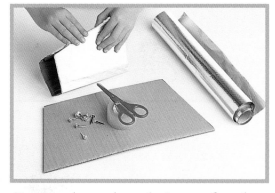

Cut two boat-shaped pieces of card to fit around your wrists. Cover each one with foil and tape the ends together. Decorate with fasteners.

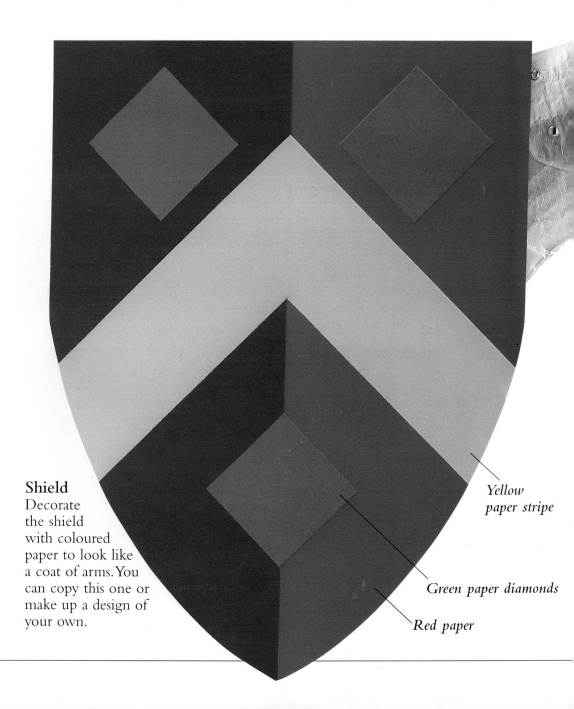

**Shield**
Decorate the shield with coloured paper to look like a coat of arms. You can copy this one or make up a design of your own.

*Yellow paper stripe*

*Green paper diamonds*

*Red paper*

**Decorate the helmet with a mini shield bearing your coat of arms.**

## Helmet
The helmet should fit comfortably over your head and sit on your shoulders.

*Slits for eye-holes*

## Dagger
The dagger can be worn slung from your belt. See page 44 for more ideas.

*Straight handle decorated with black and red coloured tape*

*The dagger has a short blade*

# Ready for action
When dressing up, first put on your breastplate, then your gauntlets, and finally your helmet. You can make arm and shoulder plates and leg guards in the same way as the gauntlets.

*Shoulder plate fixed to breast plate with sticky tape*

## Breastplate
The breastplate will slip over your head more easily if you loosen the string ties on either side.

## Sword
The sword has a long blade and a curved black guard.

*Paper fasteners look like studs*

*String tie for fastening the sides of the breastplate*

## Gauntlet
These are decorated with paper fasteners.

*Smaller version of the shield's coat of arms*

*Dark gloves complete the gauntlet*

# FIENDISH DEVIL

On the days when you feel like being really devilish, this is the costume for you. Like many successful costumes it relies on a simply decorated T-shirt and a few cunning accessories for its effect; in this case curved horns and a pointed tail. You will need a really big T-shirt to decorate; it should be long enough to reach your thighs.

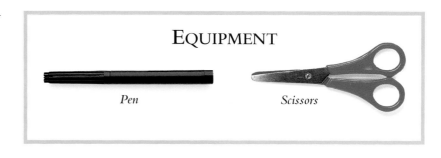

EQUIPMENT

*Pen*  *Scissors*

## You will need

*Red fabric*

*PVA glue*

*Wire*

*Safety pin*

*Orange and yellow felt*

*Red T-shirt*

*Red card*

*Hair-band*

## Decorating the T-shirt

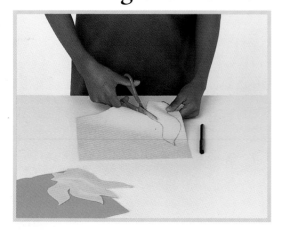

## Horns

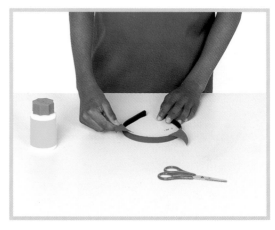

1 Draw flame shapes on pieces of felt and cut them out. Make the orange flames smaller and narrower than the yellow ones.

2 Glue yellow flames along the bottom of the T-shirt, then glue the orange ones on top. Do the same with the sleeves and shoulders.

Draw two small, curved horns on the red card and cut them out. Carefully glue them to the front of the headband, as shown.

## Pointed tail

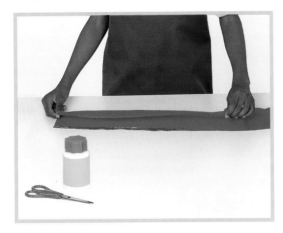

1 Cut out a strip of fabric 100 cm x 10 cm. Fold the fabric in half (100 cm x 5 cm), right side in. Glue the long edges together like a tube.

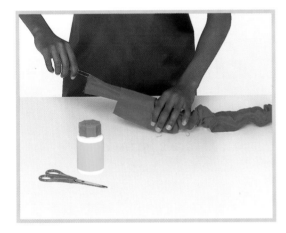

2 When the glue is dry, attach a safety pin to one end of the tail. Thread the pin through the tube to turn the fabric the right way out.

3 Thread 65 cm of wire inside the tail. Cut out two triangles and glue them together over one end of the tube and glue the other end shut.

## Feeling devilish

To complete the costume, attach the tail to the back of the T-shirt with a large safety pin and pull on a pair of red tights.

**Horns**
The curved horns are made of red card stuck to the front of a hair-band.

*Make two extra-long flames to stick to the shoulders of the T-shirt.*

**T-shirt**
A large, red T-shirt is decorated with yellow and orange felt flames.

*Two triangles of red card glued together*

*Attach the tail to the T-shirt with a safety pin.*

**Pointed tail**
Scrunch the fabric up as you thread the wire into the tail, to make it look pleated.

# HAIRY DISGUISES

For a complete change of face, why not make yourself a bushy beard and bristling moustache? Or hide your own hair under a hat and grow some chunky plaits? Here you can make both these hairy disguises, as well as a useful collection of false moustaches.

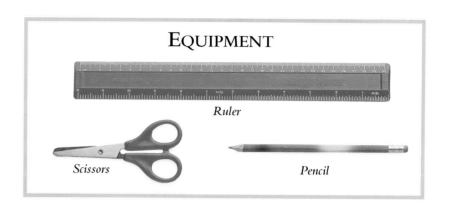

**EQUIPMENT**

*Ruler*

*Scissors*

*Pencil*

## You will need

For the plaits

*Hat*

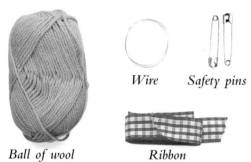

*Wire*　*Safety pins*

*Ball of wool*　*Ribbon*

For the beard and moustache

*Ball of wool*

*PVA glue*　*Thin, white card*　*Narrow elastic*

For card moustaches

*Thin, black card*

## Card moustache

Fold the black card in half. Draw half a moustache shape, as shown, next to the fold. Cut out the shape and then open out the moustache.

2 Cut pieces of wool twice the length you want the beard. Loop 3 pieces of wool at a time around the lower part of the mouth piece and tie.

## Woolly beard

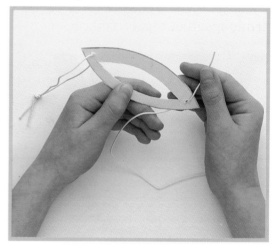

1 Cut out a mouth piece, as shown. Make a small hole at each side, then thread a piece of elastic through each hole and tie it into a loop.

3 For the moustache, cut shorter lengths of wool. Lay them across the top of the mouth piece and tie them in place with a piece of wool.

# Chunky plaits

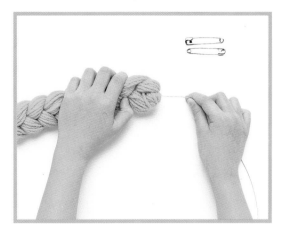

1 Cut 40 pieces of wool the length you want each plait to be. Split the wool into three bunches. Tie them firmly together at one end, as shown.

2 Plait the wool, starting from where it is tied together. Tie the other end of the plait tightly, to stop it from unravelling.

3 Thread some wire through each plait. Pin the finished ends inside the hat with a safety pin. Tie bows around the other ends of the plaits.

## Cover-ups

You can add other features, such as a hat, specs, or scarf, to complete your disguise. Turn to page 44 for more costume ideas to wear with the moustaches, beards, and plaits.

**Long and pointed moustache**

**Curly moustache**

*Adapt the nose clip to fit your nose.*

**Small moustache**

**Moustaches**
The moustaches vary in shape but are all made from black card.

*Wire in the plait makes it bend into funny shapes.*

**Chunky plaits**
By using different coloured wool or other hats, you can create a whole new costume.

*Elastic loops*

*Gingham bow*

**Woolly beard**
Hook the loops of elastic around your ears to keep the bushy beard and moustache in place.

39

# SPECS AND SHADES

Spectacles are one of the best instant disguises as they alter the appearance of your face. You can become a glittering rock star, or transform yourself into a pop-eyed mad professor. Just trace off the patterns below and transfer them on to card, to create a set of basic templates for fantastic eyewear.

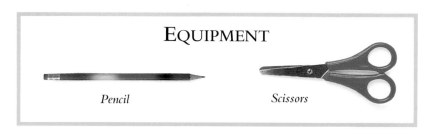

## EQUIPMENT

Pencil

Scissors

## You will need

Coloured sequins

Sticky tape

Narrow elastic

PVA glue

Felt pens

Drinking straws

Tubes of glitter

Feathers

Coloured card

Clear and coloured acetate

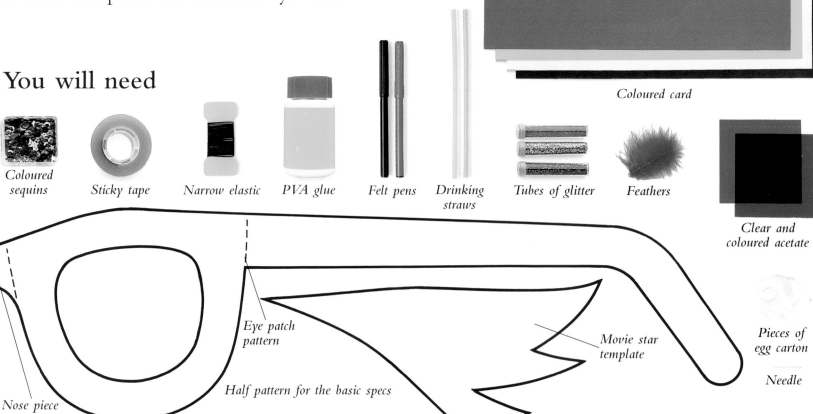

Nose piece

Eye patch pattern

Half pattern for the basic specs

Movie star template

Pieces of egg carton

Needle

## Basic specs

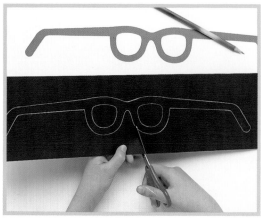

## Eye patch

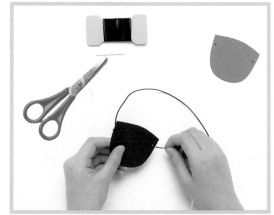

1 Draw around the basic specs template on black card. Carefully cut out the spectacles and fold back the arms.

2 Cut out two pieces of coloured acetate slightly larger than the eye-holes in the frames. Tape them in place on the back of the frames.

Draw and cut out a black card eye patch using the pattern and make two holes in it. Thread some elastic through the holes and tie the ends.

# Pop-out eyes

# Rock star shades

1 Make a pair of plain specs with clear acetate lenses. Cut out two sections of egg carton and draw an eye on the top of each of them.

2 Cut two spirals out of white card, as shown. Glue one end of each spiral to the back of an eyeball and the other end to the acetate lens.

Add the wings to the template before drawing around it. Glue glitter and sequins to the frames and make lenses from coloured acetate.

**Red shades**
Give your basic specs red lenses to see things in a different light.

*Red lenses*    *Black frames*

*Knotted end of elastic*

**Pirate's eye patch**
Eye patches come in very handy for pirate costumes.

# Glasses gallery
Decide what character you want to be and make your eyewear accordingly. Experiment with the shapes of the frames and use coloured acetate to cunningly disguise the colour of your eyes.

**Masquerade**
To make a party mask, draw around the specs template without the arms. Cut out eye-holes and decorate with coloured paper, feathers, and sequins.

*Feathers taped to outer edges*

*Tape the mask to a drinking straw*

**Pop-out eyes**
These specs make a useful addition to a mad professor's costume.

*Card spiral glued to clear acetate*

*Egg carton eyes*

*Red frames*

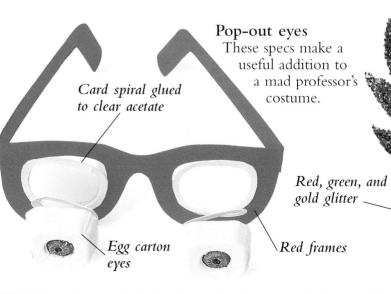

**Rock star shades**
Great for rock stars, these specs are very glittery.

*Sequins*

*Red, green, and gold glitter*

# JEWEL BOX

You can add some sparkle to any costume with this glittering range of jewellery. If you can't buy the gemstones shown below, make your own from small, round sweets covered with silver, gold, or coloured foil. Save the foil wrappers from chocolate bars and sweets.

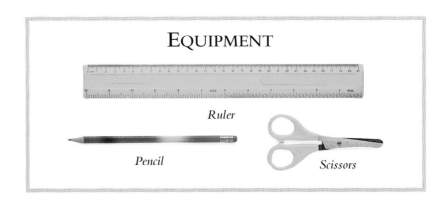

**EQUIPMENT**

Ruler

Pencil

Scissors

## You will need

Corrugated card

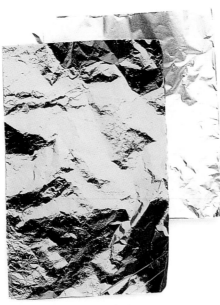

Gold and silver foil

Garden cane for wand

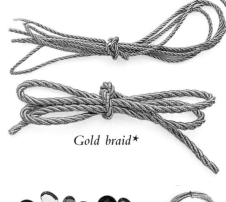

Thick string

Gold braid★

PVA glue and spatula

Flat-backed glass gemstones★

Thin wire for necklaces

Sticky tape

## Making the jewels

1 Draw the jewellery shapes you want to make on corrugated card, using household objects as templates. Then cut them out.

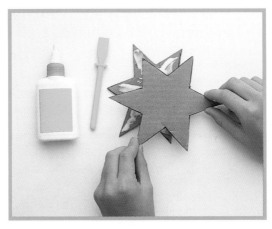

2 For big jewels, such as a star for a wand or a medallion, cut out two large stars or circles and glue them together, to make them stronger.

3 Spread glue over the card shapes and stick pieces of string to them in circles or tight spirals. Put the shapes to one side until the glue dries.

4 Cover each shape with foil, folding it to the back and gluing it down. Press the foil over the string so the pattern shows through.

5 Glue glass gemstones to the shapes for decoration. Use a large gem in the centre of big shapes and glue smaller gems around the edges.

6 For a necklace, cut pieces of thin wire and bend them into loops. Tape a loop to the back of each jewel and thread the braid through the loops.

# Glittering collection

You can use your jewels in endless different ways: thread them on to braid to make regal necklaces, belts, and medallions; glue them to earring or brooch backs; or attach them to plain rings for a sparkling transformation.

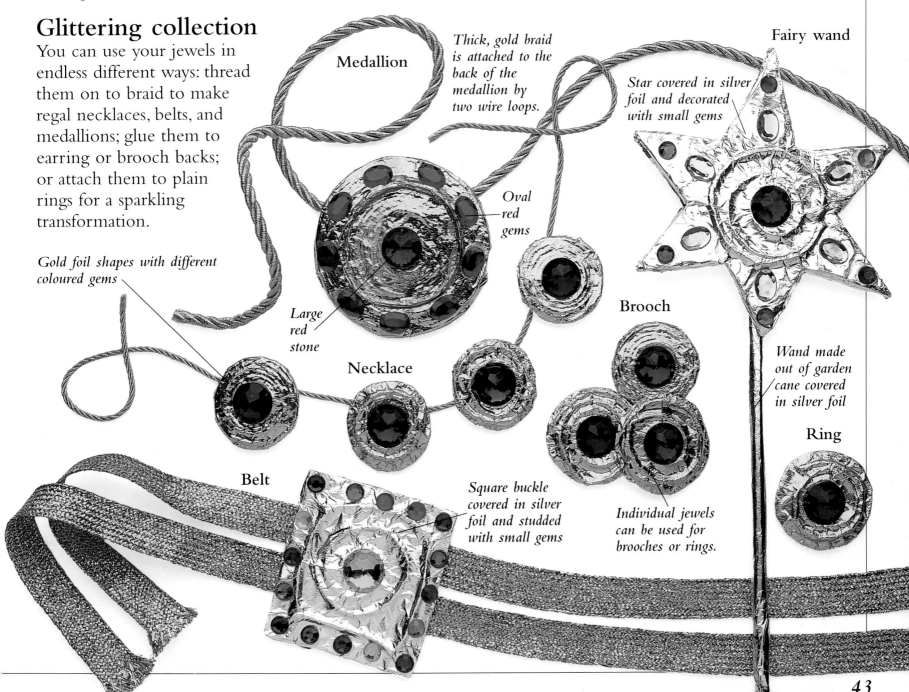

*Medallion*

*Thick, gold braid is attached to the back of the medallion by two wire loops.*

*Fairy wand*

*Star covered in silver foil and decorated with small gems*

*Oval red gems*

*Gold foil shapes with different coloured gems*

*Large red stone*

*Necklace*

*Brooch*

*Wand made out of garden cane covered in silver foil*

*Ring*

*Belt*

*Square buckle covered in silver foil and studded with small gems*

*Individual jewels can be used for brooches or rings.*

# COSTUME PARADE

You have made masks, hats, cloaks, tunics, and full outfits. Here, and over the page, you can see how simple accessories can complete an array of dazzling costumes.

Black gloves

Cloak (page 28)

Hat (page 14)

Wand

Long black T-shirt

*Ghost costume (page 20)*

*Chain*

*Black tights*

*Black tights*

Ghoulish ghost

Starry witch

Orange trousers and sweatshirt

Mask (page 6)

Mask (page 6)

Feathered cape (page 28)

Mask (page 6)

*Paper fringes tied around wrists and ankles*

Cape (page 28)

Socks on hands

*Pink T-shirt*

*Webbed feet cut out of yellow card and taped around ankles*

*Yellow tights*

Green tights

Wild lion

Evil insect

Exotic bird

44

Costume
(page 18)

Shoulder guards
made from
coloured card

Leg guards
made in
same way
as gauntlets

Gauntlets
(see armour,
page 34)

Feet (see horse's
hooves, page 10)

Space-age robot

Moustache
(page 38)

Hat
(page 14)

Star-shaped
badge
(page 42)

Smart sheriff

Jewels
(page 42)

Rock star
shades
(page 40)

Gold
shirt

Glamorous movie star

Hat
(page 14)

Red foam
ball nose

Ra-ra skirt
(page 26) worn
as neck ruff

Cheerful clown

Pop-out eyes
(page 40)

Hair
spiked
with gel

Yellow
overalls

Mad professor

Starry
headband
(page 14)

Starry wand
(page 42)

Starry
headband
(page 14)

Transparent cape
(page 28)

Skirt
(page 26)

Good fairy

Devil costume
(page 36)

Cape
(page 28)

Trident

Red tights

Fiendish devil

Bandaged head
(page 20)

Tattered
clothes

Bandaged arm
and hand

Bandaged
feet

Horror mummy

# COSTUME PARADE

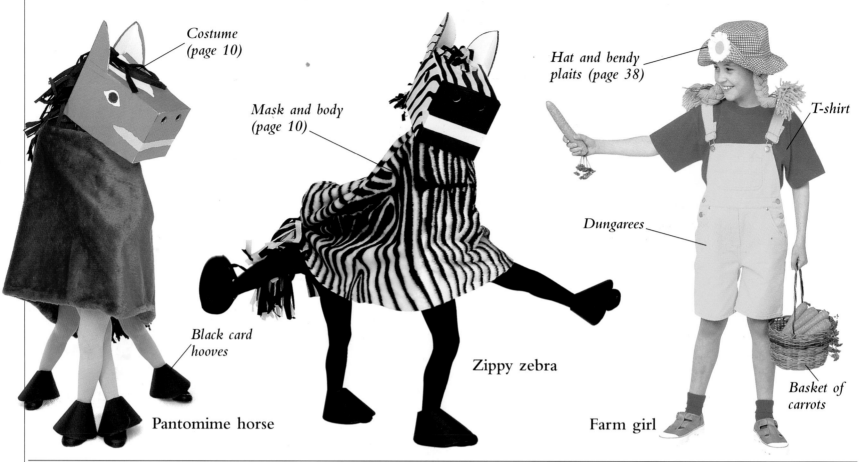

*Costume (page 10)*

*Mask and body (page 10)*

*Hat and bendy plaits (page 38)*

*T-shirt*

*Dungarees*

*Black card hooves*

Zippy zebra

*Basket of carrots*

Pantomime horse

Farm girl

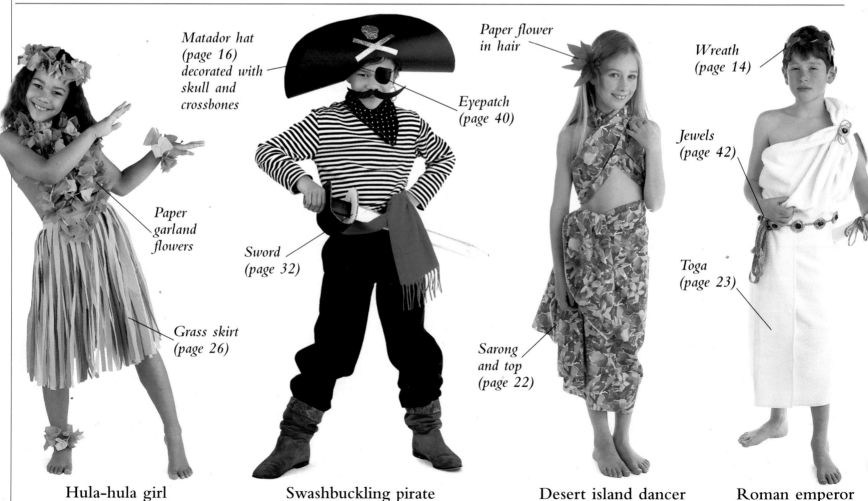

*Matador hat (page 16) decorated with skull and crossbones*

*Paper flower in hair*

*Wreath (page 14)*

*Eyepatch (page 40)*

*Jewels (page 42)*

*Paper garland flowers*

*Sword (page 32)*

*Grass skirt (page 26)*

*Sarong and top (page 22)*

*Toga (page 23)*

Hula-hula girl

Swashbuckling pirate

Desert island dancer

Roman emperor

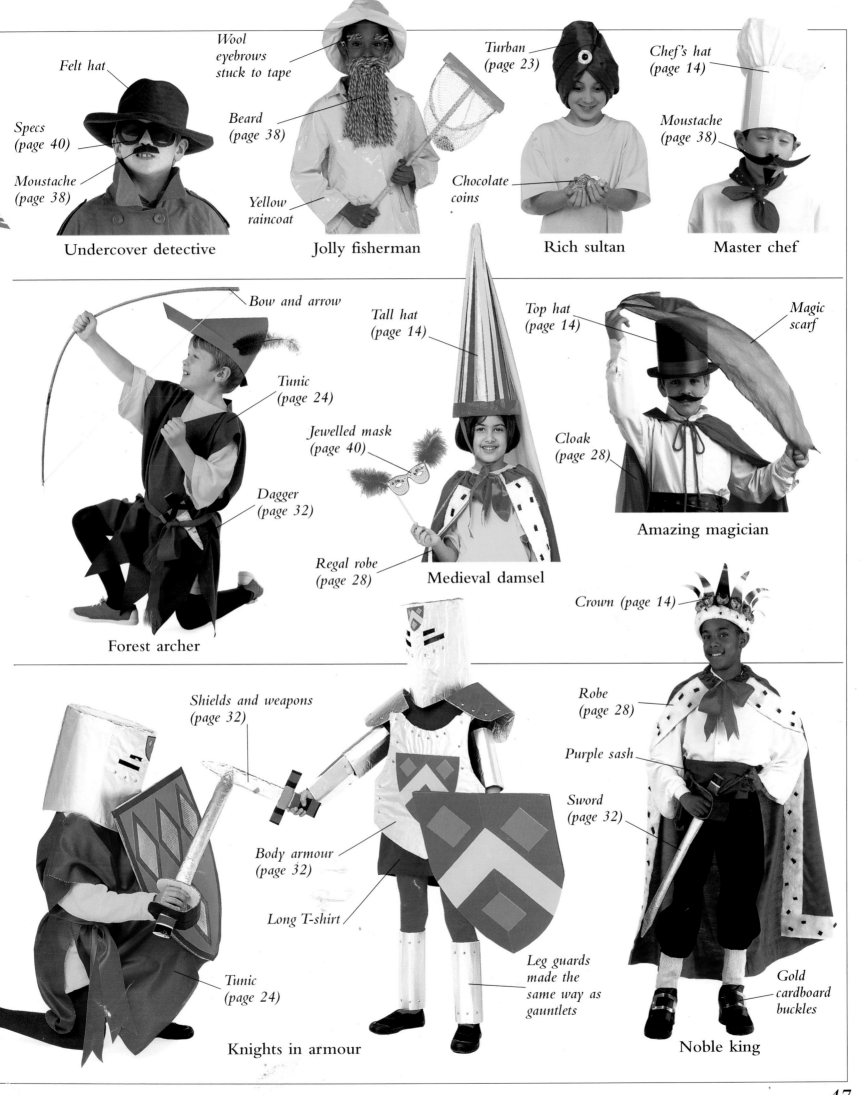

*Felt hat*

*Specs
(page 40)*

*Moustache
(page 38)*

Undercover detective

*Wool
eyebrows
stuck to tape*

*Beard
(page 38)*

*Yellow
raincoat*

Jolly fisherman

*Turban
(page 23)*

*Chocolate
coins*

Rich sultan

*Chef's hat
(page 14)*

*Moustache
(page 38)*

Master chef

*Bow and arrow*

*Tunic
(page 24)*

*Dagger
(page 32)*

Forest archer

*Tall hat
(page 14)*

*Jewelled mask
(page 40)*

*Regal robe
(page 28)*

Medieval damsel

*Top hat
(page 14)*

*Magic
scarf*

*Cloak
(page 28)*

Amazing magician

*Crown (page 14)*

*Robe
(page 28)*

*Purple sash*

*Sword
(page 32)*

*Gold
cardboard
buckles*

Noble king

*Shields and weapons
(page 32)*

*Body armour
(page 32)*

*Long T-shirt*

*Tunic
(page 24)*

*Leg guards
made the
same way as
gauntlets*

Knights in armour

# INDEX

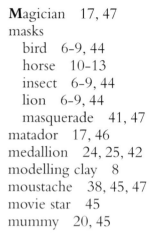
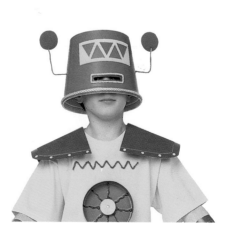